Walker Books is grateful for permission to reproduce the following:

"Five Little Monsters" from *Blackberry Ink* by Eve Merriam, © 1985 by Eve Merriam. "Toaster Time" from *There Is No Rhyme For Silver* by Eve Merriam, © 1962, 1990 by Eve Merriam. Both are reprinted by permission of Marian Reiner.

"Joyful" from *From Summer to Summer* by Rose Burgunder, © 1965 by Rose Styron. Used by permission of Viking Penguin, a division of Penguin Books USA Inc.

"Mix a Pancake" is used by permission of Simon & Schuster Books for Young Readers, an imprint of Simon & Schuster Children's Publishing Division.

Acknowledgements:

Each story in this collection has been previously published by Walker Books as a self-contained volume, except:

First published 1998 by Walker Books Ltd, 87 Vauxhall Walk, London SE11 5HJ

Text © year of publication individual authors   Illustrations © year of publication individual illustrators
Main cover illustration and title page illustration © 1985 Helen Oxenbury
All other cover illustrations taken from the books represented in this treasury

10 9 8 7 6 5 4 3 2 1

Printed in Italy

British Library Cataloguing in Publication Data
A catalogue record for this book is available from the British Library.

ISBN 0-7445-6104-3

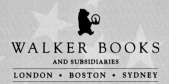

WALKER BOOKS
AND SUBSIDIARIES
LONDON • BOSTON • SYDNEY

STORIES AND FUN FOR THE VERY YOUNG

CONTENTS

Maisy's Colours

by Lucy Cousins

white dressing gown

blue sea

yellow sand

brown horse

green train

pink ears

purple horse

red coat

black spots

orange lolly

Being Together

Telling a secret,
Listening with care,

Bending down low,
Stretching high in the air.

Dancing to music,
Feeling the beat,

Lying flat on our backs
And kicking our feet.

by Shirley Hughes

Laughing,
(Always a good thing to do),

Reading out loud,
Reading to you.

Sharing a sandwich,
A new place to hide.

Love and kisses
And two smiles wide!

Getting Dressed

T-shirt

shorts

scarf

gloves

coat

sandals

sun-hat

boots

dress

Who is dressed for a hot day?

by Catherine and Laurence Anholt

vest

jumper

cardigan

pants

trousers

socks

shoes

Who is dressed for a cold day?

TOM AND PIPPO IN THE GARDEN

by Helen Oxenbury

I often take Pippo
into the garden.
He likes to ride in
my wheelbarrow.

I take him round the paths and bump
him down the steps. Pippo likes
to be bumped.

When we've had enough, I
give him his dinner. Pippo
makes a mess
when he eats.

He gets food all
over his face. So I have to
wipe him with a flannel.

When I hear Mummy calling, I make a little
bed for Pippo so he can have a sleep
while I eat my lunch.

After lunch, when we want to play, that cat is asleep in my wheelbarrow.

We have to shoo him out.

Then I take Pippo round and round the garden until it is time to go in for tea.

17

Bumps-a-daisy

Eyes,

nose,

hands,

knees,

by Colin and Jacqui Hawkins

and *bumps-a-daisy!*

NUMBERS

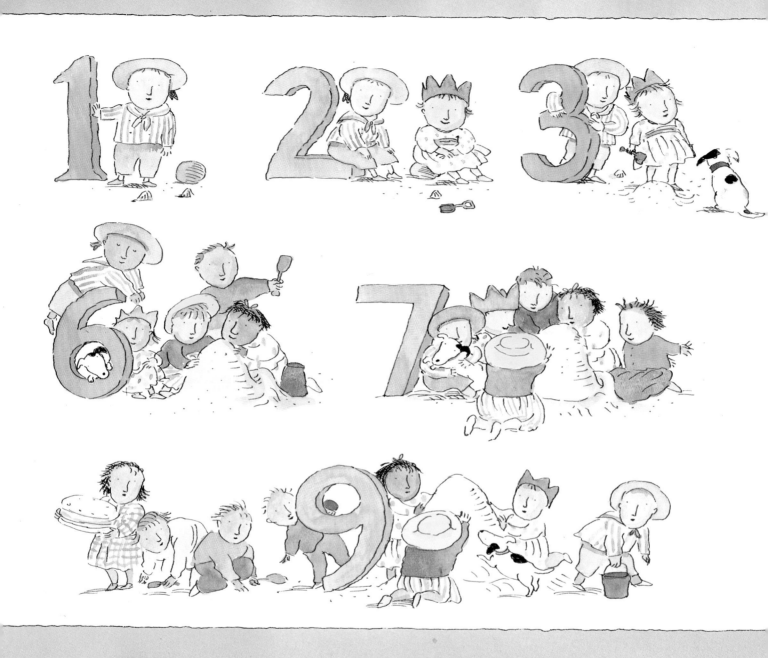

ONE, Two, three, four, five,
Once I caught a fish alive,
Six, seven, eight, nine, ten,
Then I let it go again.

illustrated by Charlotte Voake

Why did you let it go?
Because it bit my finger so.
Which finger did it bite?
This little finger on the right.

I LIKE BOOKS

I like books.
Funny books
and scary books.
Fairy tales and
nursery rhymes.
Comic books and
colouring books.
Fat books
and thin books.

by Anthony Browne

Books about
dinosaurs,
and books about
monsters.
Counting books
and alphabet
books.

Books about space,
and books
about pirates.
Song books
and strange books.

Yes, I really
do like books.

Pets
by Louise Voce

dog

goldfish

hamster

gerbil

rabbit

mouse

guinea-pig

budgie

tortoise

cat

Mum's Home

Mum's home.

And what else?

Have a banana …

by Jan Ormerod

Things for a baby.

What's in her basket?

Dig deep.   Blow Mum's nose.

and a snooze.

Hey Diddle, Diddle

illustrated by Rosemary Wells

Hey diddle, diddle,

the cat and the fiddle,

The cow jumped over the moon;

The little dog laughed

to see such fun,

And the dish ran away

with the spoon.

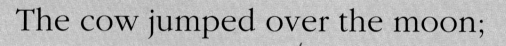

abc

illustrated by Ian Beck

Aa

alligator

Bb

bear

Cc

camel

Gg
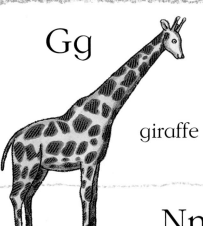
giraffe

Hh

hippopotamus

Ii
iguana

Nn

newt

Oo

ostrich

Pp
penguin

Tt

tiger

Uu

unicorn

Vv
vulture

Ww
walrus

Dd dolphin

Ee elephant

Ff flamingos

Jj jaguar

Kk kangaroo

Ll lion

Mm monkey

Qq quail

Rr rhinoceros

Ss sea-lion

Xx x-ray fish

Yy yak

Zz zebra

Joyful

and other poems

illustrated by
Arnold Lobel

Higglety, Pigglety, Pop!

Higglety, pigglety, pop!
The dog has eaten the mop;
  The pig's in a hurry,
  The cat's in a flurry,
Higglety, pigglety, pop!

Samuel Goodrich

32

Joyful

A summer day is full of ease,
  a bank is full of money,
  our lilac bush is full of bees,
and I am full of honey.

Rose Burgunder

Four Seasons

Spring is showery,
  flowery, bowery.

Summer: hoppy,
  choppy, poppy.

Autumn: wheezy,
  sneezy, freezy.

Winter: slippy,
  drippy, nippy.

Anonymous

Toddlerobics

by Zita Newcome

Hats off, coats off, all rush in,
everybody ready for toddler gym!

Heads and shoulders, knees and toes.
Eyes and ears, mouth and nose.

Flap your arms up and down.
Lift your feet off the ground.

Stretch up high and touch the sky,
bend down low and touch your toes.

Lift that rattle in the air,
shake it, shake it, everywhere!

Clap your hands, stamp your feet.
Nod your head, dance to the beat.

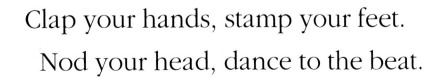

All join together to make a puffer train,

stretch out your arms and zoom like a plane.

Make a circle, ring a ring o' roses.

Let's bump bottoms, let's rub noses.

Sshhh! On tiptoes, quiet as a mouse.

Now great big steps all round the house.

Turning, twirling, like a spinning top.

Bump on your bottom when it's time to stop.

Wriggle your toes, crawl like a cat,

now lie down and stretch out flat.

Toddlerobics is lots of fun.
See you next week, everyone!

Smart Aunties

by Nick Sharratt

When my seven smart aunties came for the day,

Auntie Sue wore blue,

Auntie Dot wore spots,

Auntie Etta wore a sweater,

Auntie Tracey
wore something
lacy,

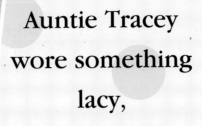

Auntie Molly
had a brolly,

Auntie Pat had
a flowery hat,

and Auntie
Madge had a cap
with a badge ...

Bye bye, Aunties!

because she
was driving
the coach.

Pat-A-Cake

Pat-a-cake, pat-a-cake,
baker's man,
Bake me a cake
as fast as you can.
Pat it, and prick it,
and mark it with b,
And put it in the oven
for baby and me!

illustrated by Tony Kenyon

Let's make a noise

Let's make a noise like a dog.

WOOF

Let's make a noise like a train.

TOOT, TOOT

Let's make a noise like a cat.

MEOW

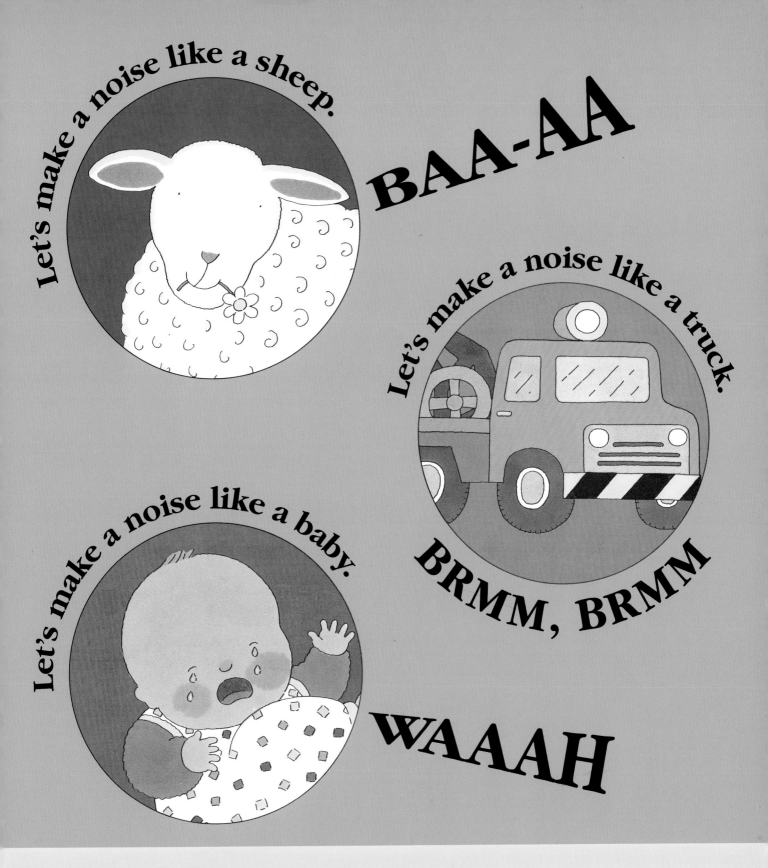

Let's make a noise like a sheep.

BAA-AA

Let's make a noise like a truck.

BRMM, BRMM

Let's make a noise like a baby.

WAAAH

by Amy MacDonald
illustrated by Maureen Roffey

43

Read-Aloud Rhymes

Toaster Time

Tick tick tick tick
  tick tick tick
Toast up a sandwich
  quick quick quick
Hamwich
Or jamwich
Lick lick lick!

Tick tick tick tick
  tick tick––stop!

POP!

Eve Merriam

Mix a Pancake

Mix a pancake,
Stir a pancake,
Pop it in the pan;
Fry the pancake,
Toss the pancake –
Catch it if you can.

Christina Rossetti

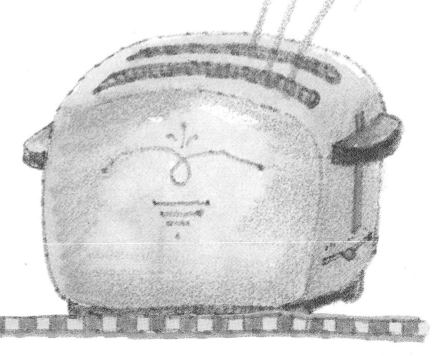

illustrated by Marc Brown

FIVE LITTLE MONSTERS

Five little monsters
By the light of the moon
Stirring pudding with
A wooden pudding spoon.
The first one says,
"It mustn't be runny."
The second one says,
"That would make it taste funny."
The third one says,
"It mustn't be lumpy."
The fourth one says,
"That would make me grumpy."
The fifth one smiles,
Hums a little tune,
And licks all the drippings
 From the wooden
  pudding spoon.

Eve Merriam

DAVY DUMPLING

Davy Davy Dumpling,
 Boil him in the pot;
Sugar him and butter him,
 And eat him while he's hot.

Anonymous

Lizzie and her kitty

by David Martin　　*illustrated by Debi Gliori*

Where is Lizzie?
Lizzie's in her chair.

Where is Lizzie's pudding?
Dripping from her hair.

Where is Lizzie's kitty?
Kitty's on the floor.

Kitty's licking pudding
And hoping for some more.

Now where is Lizzie?
Lizzie's at the sink.

She's turning on the water
So she can get a drink.

Now where is kitty?
With Lizzie in her chair.

And what is kitty doing?
Licking Lizzie's hair.

Billy's Boot

Let's put the toys away, Billy.

Billy help Lily.

Spot and Slinky go in the basket, ball in basket too.

48

by Martha Alexander

It's all done, Billy.

All done!

Where's your boot, Billy?

Boot, Lily!

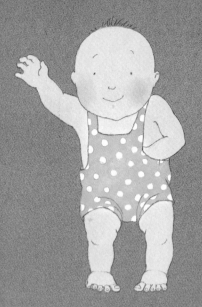

I can
by Helen Oxenbury

sit

dance

slide

run

bend

crawl

fall

jump

stretch

kick

FISHERMAN

Heave ho!
Away we go.

Rub-a-dub,
scour and scrub.

Net's full,
tug and pull.

Lower the catch,
down the hatch.

by **Paul Manning**   *illustrated by* **Nicola Bayley**

Mind that plate –
too late!

Achooo!
Wet through.

Prepare the buoy.
Land ahoy!

Heave a sigh,
home and dry.

The Wheels on the Bus

The wheels on the bus go round and round,
Round and round, round and round,
The wheels on the bus go round and round,
All day long.

The grans on the bus
go knit, knit,
knit…

The children on the bus
go wriggle, wriggle,
wriggle…

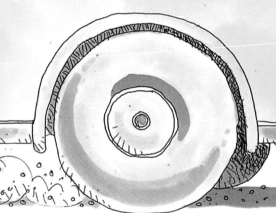

illustrated by Toni Goffe

The dads
on the bus
go nod, nod,
nod…

The mums
on the bus
go chatter, chatter,
chatter…

The wipers
on the bus
go swish, swish
swish…

The horn on the bus
goes beep, beep,
beep…

The driver on the bus
goes bother, bother,
bother…

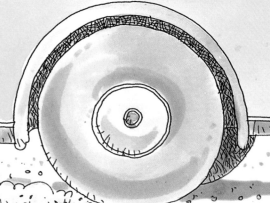

Baby Animals on the Farm

horse
and foal

sheep and
lambs

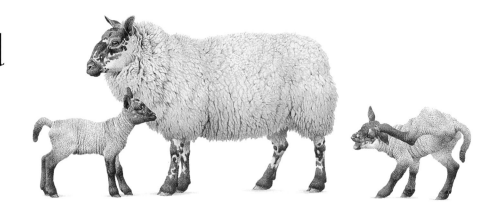

duck and

ducklings

by Kenneth Lilly

cow
and calf

pig and
piglets

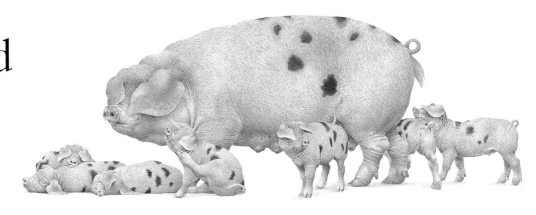

chickens
and
chicks

Hush, Little Baby

Hush, little baby, don't say a word,
Papa's going to buy you a mocking bird.

If the mocking bird won't sing,
Papa's going to buy you a diamond ring.

If the diamond ring turns to brass,
Papa's going to buy you a looking-glass.

If the looking-glass gets broke,
Papa's going to buy you a billy-goat.

If that billy-goat runs away,
Papa's going to buy you another today.

illustrated by Julie Lacome

Goodnight

Messy dinner cleared away,
Toys packed up for another day,
Now it's bathtime, taking off clothes,
Wriggly, giggly, tickly toes.

Splashy water, boats in a storm,
Out you get, cuddle up warm,
Nice clean teeth, clever baby!
Nice clean nappy, pyjamas, maybe?

Bedtime story, sleepyhead,
It's getting late, time for bed,
Goodnight, moon, shining bright,
Goodnight, room, cosy light.

Snuggle down, no need to cry,
One more song, a lullaby,
Goodnight, bear, can't help yawning,
Goodnight, baby, see you in the morning.

by Clara Vulliamy